Passing the PRINCE2 Examinations

The APM Group,
based on the original book
by Ken Bradley

London: TSO

Published by TSO (The Stationery Office) and available from:

Online
www.tsoshop.co.uk

Mail, Telephone, Fax & E-mail
TSO
PO Box 29, Norwich, NR3 1GN
Telephone orders/General enquiries: 0870 600 5522
Fax orders: 0870 600 5533
E-mail: customer.services@tso.co.uk
Textphone 0870 240 3701

TSO Shops
123 Kingsway, London, WC2B 6PQ
020 7242 6393 Fax 020 7242 6394
16 Arthur Street, Belfast BT1 4GD
028 9023 8451 Fax 028 9023 5401
71 Lothian Road, Edinburgh EH3 9AZ
0870 606 5566 Fax 0870 606 5588

TSO @ Blackwell and other Accredited Agents

The information contained in this publication is believed to be correct at the
time of manufacture. Whilst care has been taken to ensure that the information
is accurate, the publisher can accept no responsibility for any errors or
omissions or for changes to the details given.

PRINCE® is a Registered Trade Mark and a Registered Community Trade Mark
of the Office of Government Commerce, and is Registered in the U.S. Patent
and Trademark Office

The PRINCE2 Cityscape logo ™ is a Trade Mark of the Office of Government
Commerce, and is Registered in the U.S. Patent and Trademark Office

PRINCE2 ™ is a Trade Mark of the Office of Government Commerce

A CIP catalogue record for this book is available from the British Library
A Library of Congress CIP catalogue record has been applied for

First published 2005
Fourth impression 2007

ISBN 978 0 11 330978 8

Printed in the United Kingdom by The Stationery Office, London
N5512165 C40 02/06 319042 19585

Contents

Foreword

This book is aimed at easing the path for all those intending to take the APM Group PRINCE2 foundation and practitioner examinations. Those taking the APM Group Practitioner Re-Registration Examination will find that the advice provided is equally relevant and useful. *Passing the PRINCE2 Examinations* has been updated to reflect changes to the PRINCE2 reference manual released on 31 May 2005.

Thanks go to the APM Group and the PRINCE2 Examination Board for allowing the use of PRINCE2 examination material, and Richard Pharro for his support and encouragement in getting this publication to print.

I hope you will find this book of real use in preparing for, and passing, your examinations. The royalties from this book go to the APM Group annual PRINCE2 award scheme – full details of which can be obtained from the APM Group.

This is a complementary, not a 'core', publication on PRINCE2, and therefore is not endorsed by the PRINCE2 Examination Board.

Based on an original idea by Ken Bradley

July 2005

The Foundation and Practitioner Joint Syllabus (2005)

The ticks in the right-hand columns in the syllabus below show what topics are included in the two examinations. This syllabus is correct at the time of going to press. This can be checked by accessing the www.PRINCE2.ORG website, which always contains the latest version of the syllabus.

APM GROUP

Contents

Introduction

This syllabus is designed to provide a basis for accreditation of project management professionals. The syllabus is based on the OGC publication *Managing Successful Projects with PRINCE2* (2002) and the OGC publication *Managing Successful Projects with PRINCE2* (2005) and is intended to provide a basis for setting examinations at Foundation and Practitioner levels. The following table describes the competence required at each level.

Foundation	This level is aiming to measure whether a candidate would be able to act as an informed member of a project management team on a project using the PRINCE2 method, within an environment supporting PRINCE2. To this end they need to show they understand the principles and terminology of the method. Specifically, candidates must be able to: • Describe the purpose and major content of all roles, the eight components, the eight processes, and the techniques. • State which management products are input to, output from, and updated in the eight processes, and the sub-processes of Controlling a Stage (CS) and Managing Product Delivery (MP). • State the main purpose, and key contents, of the major management products as identified in the detailed syllabus. • State the relationships between processes, deliverables, roles and the management dimensions of a project.
Practitioner	This level is aiming to measure whether a candidate would be able to apply PRINCE2 to the running and managing of a project within an environment supporting PRINCE2. To this end they need to exhibit the competence required for the Foundation qualification, and show that they can apply and tune PRINCE2 to address the needs and problems of a specific project scenario. Specifically, candidates must be able to: • Produce detailed explanations of all processes, components and techniques, and worked examples of all PRINCE2 products as they might be applied to address the particular circumstances of a given project scenario. • Demonstrate that they understand the relationships between processes, components, techniques and PRINCE2 products and can apply this understanding. • Demonstrate that they understand the reasons behind the processes, components and techniques of PRINCE2, and that they understand the principles underpinning these elements. • Demonstrate their ability to tune PRINCE2 to different project circumstances.

The syllabus will also inform the design, development and use of training materials and courses aimed at raising an individual's understanding of and competence in the project management approach as described in *Managing Successful Projects with PRINCE2*. The syllabus has been designed with ease of reference, extensibility and ease of maintenance in mind. The structure of the syllabus is depicted in Figure 1.

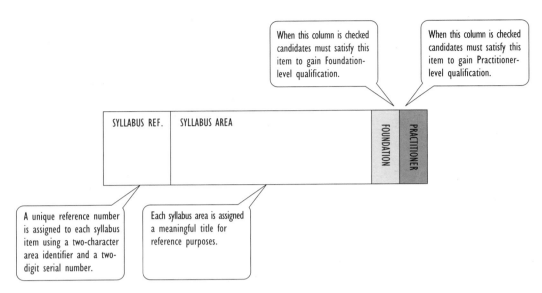

Figure 1 Syllabus Structure

Syllabus

Syllabus Reference	Syllabus Area	Foundation	Practitioner

Overview and principles

				Foundation	Practitioner
OV	01	Candidates must be able to identify the typical characteristics of a project.		✓	✓
OV	02	Candidates must be able to identify the benefits of a structured approach to project management.		✓	✓
OV	03	Candidates must be able to identify the relationship between the project environment and the daily business of an organisation.		✓	✓
OV	04	Candidates must be able to identify the differences between the project life cycle and the product lifespan.		✓	✓
OV	05	Candidates must be able to identify what part of a product lifespan is covered by PRINCE2.		✓	✓
OV	06	Candidates must be able to identify the main elements of PRINCE2, including the eight processes, the components and the techniques.		✓	✓
OV	07	Candidates must understand PRINCE2 terminology, including customer, supplier, user, product, Business Case, exception and stage.		✓	✓
OV	08	Candidates must be able to justify the use of PRINCE2 for a given project scenario, and explain the benefits of its application to that scenario.			✓

Organisation

				Foundation	Practitioner
OR	01	Candidates must be able to describe the purpose of organisation.		✓	✓

Syllabus Reference		Syllabus Area	Foundation	Practitioner
OR	02	Candidates must be able to identify the four layers in the project organisation structure, including the differences between the management and the direction of a project.	✓	✓
OR	03	Candidates must understand the differing Business, User and Supplier interests of participating parties in a project, and how these will be represented within the standard project organisation structure.	✓	✓
OR	04	Candidates must be able to identify the products of organisation.	✓	✓
OR	05	Candidates must understand the purpose and responsibilities of the Project Board, Project Manager, Project Assurance, Team Manager and Project Support, and be able to identify the acceptable consolidations or sharing of roles.	✓	✓
OR	06	Candidates must be able to produce a design for an appropriate organisation, applying all roles as identified in PRINCE2, with explanations of the responsibilities of each role and of the reporting and information flow relationships between roles for a given project scenario.		✓
OR	07	Candidates must be able to apply and explain acceptable role consolidations/sharing and their resultant organisation structure to a given project scenario.		✓
OR	08	Candidates must be able to produce Role Descriptions for the Project Board, Project Manager, Team Manager, Project Assurance and Project Support tuned for the particular needs of a given project scenario.		✓

Business Case

			Foundation	Practitioner
BN	01	Candidates must be able to describe the fundamental importance of the benefits focus of PRINCE2 in project management.	✓	✓
BN	02	Candidates must be able to describe the purpose of the Business Case.	✓	✓
BN	03	Candidates must understand the contents of a Business Case, where in the eight processes these are created, updated and monitored, and which roles are responsible for this work.	✓	✓
BN	04	Candidates must be able to identify the factors in a given project scenario that would be considered in the development of the Business Case.		✓
BN	05	Candidates must be able to show how a Business Case would be created, updated, used and modified within the PRINCE2 processes, and how the various roles would be involved, by application to a given project scenario.		✓
BN	06	Candidates must be able to create, modify or discuss a Business Case from information provided in a given project scenario.		✓
BN	07	Candidates must be able to identify the relationship between the Business Case and other PRINCE2 products and components in any given project scenario.		✓
BN	08	Candidates must be able to state benefits in measurable terms.		✓

Knowledge of the Business Case contents excludes any detailed knowledge of how to perform an Investment Appraisal or techniques such as sensitivity analysis and GAP analysis.

Syllabus Reference		Syllabus Area	Foundation	Practitioner

Controls

CO	01	Candidates must be able to describe the purpose of Controls.	✓	✓
CO	02	Candidates must be able to identify the products involved in the controlled start of a project and understand the purpose and contents of each product.	✓	✓
CO	03	Candidates must be able to identify the products used to manage the controlled progress in a project and understand the purpose and contents of each product.	✓	✓
CO	04	Candidates must understand the purpose, types and application of tolerance.	✓	✓
CO	05	Candidates must understand the reasons for breaking a project into stages and understand the difference between management and technical stages.	✓	✓
CO	06	Candidates must be able to identify the products involved in bringing a project to a controlled close and understand the purpose and contents of each product.	✓	✓
CO	07	Candidates must be able to describe the Controls responsibilities and activities of the various PRINCE2 roles within each of the eight processes.	✓	✓
CO	08	Candidates must be able to create, modify or discuss any of the products of Controls in a given project scenario.		✓
CO	09	Candidates must be able to describe in detail each control, its purpose and content, the relevant processes involved in its application, and which roles are involved via application to any given project scenario.		✓
CO	10	Candidates must be able to apply any of the controls defined by PRINCE2 to a given project scenario.		✓
CO	11	Candidates must be able to identify the relationship between Controls and other PRINCE2 components within any given project scenario.		✓

Change Control

CC	01	Candidates must be able to describe the purpose of Change Control.	✓	✓
CC	02	Candidates must be able to identify the products and general administration of Change Control, and understand the content and purpose of a Project Issue, Request for Change, and Off-specification.	✓	✓
CC	03	Candidates must understand the link between Change Control and Configuration Management.	✓	✓
CC	04	Candidates must understand the PRINCE2 Change Control technique.	✓	✓
CC	05	Candidates must understand the Change Control responsibilities and activities of the various PRINCE2 roles within each of the eight processes.	✓	✓
CC	06	Candidates must be able to create, modify or discuss any of the products of Change Control in a given project scenario.		✓
CC	07	Candidates must be able to apply Change Control to a given project scenario.		✓

Syllabus Reference		Syllabus Area	Foundation	Practitioner
CC	08	Candidates must be able to apply the Change Control technique to a given project scenario.		✓
CC	09	Candidates must be able to discuss the factors determining escalation of Project Issues to the Project Board, identify the processes involved and create/ discuss the products required, for any given project scenario.		✓
CC	10	Candidates must be able to discuss the factors affecting the application of the Change Budget and the possible appointment of a Change Authority in any given project scenario.		✓
CC	11	Candidates must be able to identify the relationship between Change Control and other PRINCE2 components within any given project scenario.		✓

The Management of Risk

			Foundation	Practitioner
RK	01	Candidates must be able to describe the purpose of the Management of Risk.	✓	✓
RK	02	Candidates must understand the purpose of the Risk Log, where within the eight processes it is created and updated, and the main responsibilities of the PRINCE2 roles in this regard.	✓	✓
RK	03	Candidates must be able to apply the Management of Risk to a given project scenario.		✓
RK	04	Candidates must be able to create, modify or discuss a Risk Log for a given project scenario.		✓
RK	05	Candidates must be able to demonstrate the interfaces between the Risk Log and other PRINCE2 products especially Project Issues in a given project scenario.		✓
RK	06	Candidates must be able to identify the relationship between Management of Risk and other PRINCE2 components in a given project scenario.		✓

Quality in a project environment

			Foundation	Practitioner
QU	01	Candidates must be able to describe the purpose of Quality Management.	✓	✓
QU	02	Candidates must be able to identify the products of Quality Management, and understand the purpose and content of each product.	✓	✓
QU	03	Candidates must be able to describe the importance of the customer's quality expectations.	✓	✓
QU	04	Candidates must understand the part played by a possible quality management system from the user or supplier in contributing to a Project Quality Plan.	✓	✓
QU	05	Candidates must understand the Quality Management responsibilities and activities of the various PRINCE2 roles within each of the eight processes.	✓	✓
QU	06	Candidates must understand the quality path through a project as illustrated by PRINCE2.	✓	✓

Syllabus Reference		Syllabus Area	Foundation	Practitioner
QU	07	Candidates must be able to understand the relationship between an organisation's quality assurance and the Project Assurance role.	✓	✓
QU	08	Candidates must be able to discuss the role played by Project Assurance in the various PRINCE2 processes, components and techniques.		✓
QU	09	Candidates must be able to create, modify or discuss any of the products of Quality Management in a given project scenario.		✓
QU	10	Candidates must be able to apply Quality Management to a given project scenario.		✓
QU	11	Candidates must be able to identify the relationship between Quality Management and other PRINCE2 components within any given project scenario.		✓

Candidates are not required to have any detailed understanding of ISO 9000:2000.

Plans

			Foundation	Practitioner
PL	01	Candidates must be able to describe the purpose of the Plans component.	✓	✓
PL	02	Candidates must understand the necessity for, and advantages of, producing a plan.	✓	✓
PL	03	Candidates must understand the Plans responsibilities and activities of the various PRINCE2 roles within each of the eight processes.	✓	✓
PL	04	Candidates must understand the purpose and content of the Project Plan, Stage Plan, Team Plan and Exception Plan and where in the eight processes these plans are created.	✓	✓
PL	05	Candidates must understand the interrelationship between the Project Plan, Stage Plans, Team Plans and an Exception Plan.	✓	✓
PL	06	Candidates must be able to create, modify or discuss any level of plan for any given project scenario.		✓
PL	07	Candidates must be able to demonstrate the application of the planning responsibilities as defined by PRINCE2 for any given project scenario.		✓
PL	08	Candidates must be able to apply the Plans component to a given project scenario.		✓
PL	09	Candidates must be able to identify the relationship between Plans and other PRINCE2 components within any given project scenario.		✓

Required knowledge of the techniques of network planning and Gantt charts reaches only as far as being able to identify the PRINCE2 sub-processes in which they might be created, and does not include how to create/modify or use these techniques (Practitioner level only).

Syllabus Reference		Syllabus Area	Foundation	Practitioner

Configuration management

CM	01	Candidates must be able to describe the purpose of configuration management.	✓	✓
CM	02	Candidates must understand version control and the reasons for it.	✓	✓
CM	03	Candidates must be able to identify the products of configuration management.	✓	✓
CM	04	Candidates must understand the PRINCE2 filing structure.	✓	✓
CM	05	Candidates must understand the configuration management responsibilities and activities of the various PRINCE2 roles within each of the eight processes.	✓	✓
CM	06	Candidates must understand the Configuration Librarian role, and the relationship of this role to all the other PRINCE2 defined roles.	✓	✓
CM	07	Candidates must understand the relationship between configuration management and Change Control.	✓	✓
CM	08	Candidates must understand the relationship between project configuration management and any operational configuration management.	✓	✓
CM	09	Candidates must be able to create, modify or discuss any of the products of configuration management in a given project scenario.		✓
CM	10	Candidates must be able to apply configuration management to a given project scenario.		✓
CM	11	Candidates must be able to demonstrate how to integrate the requirements of project configuration management with an existing operational configuration management environment for any given project scenario.		✓
CM	12	Candidates must be able to identify the relationship between configuration management and other PRINCE2 components within any given project scenario.		✓

Processes

PR	01	Candidates must understand the objectives, inputs and outputs of each of the eight processes, and their normal sequence.	✓	✓
PR	02	Candidates must understand the objectives, inputs and outputs of each of the sub-processes of Controlling a Stage (CS) and Managing Product Delivery (MP), and their normal sequence.	✓	✓
PR	03	Candidates must be able to describe the objectives, inputs and outputs for all of the processes and sub-processes and the main steps involved in the carrying out of each of the processes and sub-processes as described by PRINCE2.		✓
PR	04	Candidates must be able to demonstrate the application of the processes and sub-processes as described by PRINCE2, their interfaces and inter-dependencies, for any given project scenario.		✓
PR	05	Candidates must be able to describe in detail the objective, nature and relevant responsibilities of each project role in each of the processes and sub-processes.		✓

Syllabus Reference		Syllabus Area	Foundation	Practitioner
PR	06	Candidates must be able to describe in detail the passage of all PRINCE2 products through the processes and sub-processes.		✓

Product-based planning

			Foundation	Practitioner
PP	01	Candidates must understand the steps involved in product-based planning.	✓	✓
PP	02	Candidates must understand the benefits and uses of product-based planning.	✓	✓
PP	03	Candidates must understand where in the eight processes product-based planning is used as described in PRINCE2.	✓	✓
PP	04	Candidates must be able to describe the purpose and content of the three product-based planning products, and be able to describe which PRINCE2 roles should be involved in their production and use.	✓	✓
PP	05	Candidates must be able to relate the product-based planning technique and products to the sub-processes of the planning process.		✓
PP	06	Candidates must be able to create, modify or discuss a Product Breakdown Structure and Product Flow Diagram as described by PRINCE2, for a given project scenario.		✓
PP	07	Candidates must be able to create, modify or discuss a Product Description for a product identified in any given project scenario.		✓

Quality review

			Foundation	Practitioner
QR	01	Candidates must understand the purpose, and benefits of a quality review.	✓	✓
QR	02	Candidates must understand the three steps of a quality review as described in PRINCE2.	✓	✓
QR	03	Candidates must understand the purpose and content of the products used in a quality review.	✓	✓
QR	04	Candidates must understand where within the eight processes quality reviews are planned and conducted, and the various roles of the project management team involved in their planning and conduct.	✓	✓
QR	05	Candidates must understand the roles used in a quality review, and how these relate to the standard PRINCE2 roles.	✓	✓
QR	06	Candidates must be able to create, modify or discuss any of the products of quality review in a given project scenario.		✓
QR	07	Candidates must be able to apply the quality review technique to any given project scenario.		✓
QR	08	Candidates must be able to discuss in detail the links between a quality review, the processes and project management team roles, and to show how this could be applied to any given project scenario.		✓

The Foundation Examination

What is the examination?

The Foundation Examination is a one-hour, closed-book examination. It is designed to test the candidate's knowledge of the PRINCE2 method by choosing the correct answer from a selection of possible answers. There are 75 questions in all and candidates must score 38 correct answers or more to pass. There is no consolidation or carry-forward of time or scores to the Practitioner Examination – the Foundation Examination stands alone. Candidates intending to take the PRINCE2 Practitioner Examination (or any other PRINCE-related examination) must first pass the Foundation Examination.

The track record

Statistics released by the APM Group to PRINCE2 Accredited Training Organisations (ATOs) show that around 95% of all candidates pass the Foundation Examination, indicating that the level of understanding of the PRINCE2 terminology and overview of the method is high.

The Practitioner Examination requires candidates to demonstrate that they are able to apply the method to a project situation. Only around 65% of candidates taking the Registered Practitioner Examination reach the required standard, indicating that the examination is quite a tough test of their ability to take a project scenario and answer questions on how to apply the PRINCE2 method. A later section of this publication provides advice and guidance on the Practitioner Examination.

There is an interesting correlation between marks scored in the Foundation Examination and success in the Practitioner Examination – essentially the more marks scored in the Foundation Examination, the higher the success rate at practitioner level. Candidates who pass the Foundation Examination with 38–40 marks are, statistically, much less likely to pass the Practitioner Examination; those with Foundation Examination scores in excess of 70 marks almost always pass the Practitioner Examination.

The examination questions

On the following pages are examples of the questions and multiple-choice answers that make up the Foundation Examination. Do not approach the questions 'cold'; you must have done quite a bit of preparation before attempting any, otherwise you will get demoralised!

There are over 450 questions in the APM Group database from which the actual examination questions are taken. Some of the questions are very straightforward and will give you little trouble; others drill down into the method and are there to really test your knowledge. You will find that some of the possible answers posed can be eliminated with even a basic knowledge of the method.

Preparing for the examination

Success in the Foundation Examination requires a good understanding of PRINCE2 terminology, an overview of the method and the flows of information within it. The official PRINCE2 manual (*Managing Successful Projects with PRINCE2* ISBN: 0 11 330946 5), produced by the Office of Government Commerce (OGC), does not contain a single, overall, detailed process map and it is well worth studying the one shown in Figure 2 as part of your preparation for the examination.

Figure 2 takes each of the major processes and maps the flows of information and products between them.

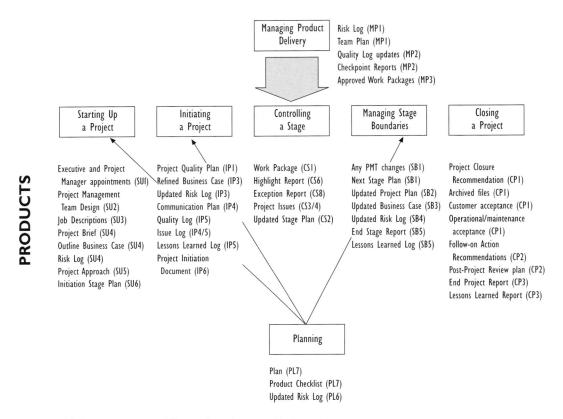

Figure 2 Major processes and flows of products and information

The acronym in brackets after each product identifies the sub-process that creates it. Remember, for the Foundation Examination, you do not need to go down to the sub-process level in most processes, only in the CS (Controlling a Stage) and MP (Managing Product Delivery) processes. As part of your preparation, try to produce your own diagram – do not simply rely on the one shown here!

Remember that the main benefit from creating your own summary process diagram will come from the research you will need to do into each process. You will not be allowed to take your summary process diagram into the Foundation Examination, but it will be a useful revision aid and helpful in structuring the content of the Practitioner Examination answers.

Technique for completing the examination

The paper contains 75 questions, most of which offer four optional answers. Occasionally there will be only two options, e.g. TRUE or FALSE. One (and only one) of the options will be the correct answer. All you have to do is put a tick in the box that corresponds to your chosen answer for that question on the appropriate row on the answer sheet that is provided.

The best technique for the Foundation Examination is to go through the paper in a first non-stop 'sweep', answering all the straightforward questions to which you know the answers; ignore any long, wordy questions or those that might need some working out. The paper may include 'negative' questions (i.e. *'Which of the following options is FALSE…'*) and you might find it easier to return to these at a later time.

When your first sweep is completed you should have most of the questions answered; typically this will take about 15–25 minutes. You can at this stage count up the number of questions you know you have answered correctly to provide a confidence boost – but beware that this might have the opposite effect!

Now return to those more obscure or difficult questions in a second sweep. Many will not be as tricky as they first appeared and, with a bit of common sense and careful reading of the question, you should be able to discount many of the options offered. This may leave you with one option that on re-examination is clearly the correct option. For other questions, you may be left with, say, two options from which you still cannot choose. Leave these and continue the second sweep. You should now feel confident that you are well beyond the pass mark and still have time to spare. Return for a third sweep through those (few) outstanding questions. Review the question and the remaining options. For some, the answer may now suggest itself. For the others, think about them again, but before time runs out, at least make a guess. You should have at least a fifty-fifty chance of being right.

Beware of changing answers you already have – general experience indicates that there are probably as many changes made from correct to incorrect answers as there are from incorrect to correct! If you need to make a change, show it clearly.

You should now be ready to try a Foundation Examination paper – if you have done your preparation work you should be feeling quite confident and ready to tackle the example examination which starts on the next page. Always plan your approach to the real examination – time the completion of the example paper that follows for no more than two days before the examination – you will then be finely honed – with just enough time to review the elements you missed out on but not too much time to cause you to lose the cutting edge you'll need for the real thing.

Good luck!

Sample Foundation Examination Paper

Multiple Choice

Instructions

---

1.   All 75 questions should be attempted.

2.   There are no trick questions.

3.   All answers are to be marked on the original examination paper.

4.   Please use a pen to mark your answers with either a ✓ or ✗.

5.   You have 1 hour for this paper.

6.   You must get 38 or more correct to pass.

Candidate Number: ....

---

1. In PRINCE2 what product is used to define the information that justifies the setting up, continuation or termination of the project?

    a)   Project Initiation Document   ☐

    b)   Business Case   ☐

    c)   End Stage Approval   ☐

    d)   Project Brief   ☐

2. Which product keeps track of Requests for Change?

    a)   Request Log   ☐

    b)   Daily Log   ☐

    c)   Quality Log   ☐

    d)   Issue Log   ☐

3. What provision in Planning can be made for implementing Requests for Change?

    a)   Project and stage tolerances   ☐

    b)   Contingency plans   ☐

    c)   A Change Budget   ☐

    d)   Adding a contingency margin to estimates   ☐

4. Fill in the missing phrase from 'a project is a management environment that is created for the purpose of delivering one or more business products according to …'

    a)   the Customer's Needs   ☐

    b)   an Agreed Contract   ☐

    c)   the Project Plan   ☐

    d)   a specified Business Case   ☐

5. In what sequence would (a) the Project Initiation Document, (b) the Project Mandate and (c) the Project Brief appear in a PRINCE2 project?

    a)   a, b, c   ☐

    b)   b, c, a   ☐

    c)   c, a, b   ☐

    d)   c, b, a   ☐

6.   Which would require the production of an Exception Report?

    a)   When a Project Issue is received ☐

    b)   When a Project Board member raises a complaint ☐

    c)   When a Request for Change or Off-Specification has been received ☐

    d)   When the current forecasts for the end of the stage deviate beyond the delegated tolerance bounds ☐

7.   Which statement is NOT a fundamental principle of 'Closing a Project'?

'A clear end to a project ...'

    a)   provides a useful opportunity to take stock of achievements ☐

    b)   provides an opportunity to ensure that all unachieved goals and objectives are identified ☐

    c)   provides the opportunity to evaluate achievement of all the expected benefits ☐

    d)   is always more successful than the natural tendency to drift into operational management ☐

8.   What is the more common term used in PRINCE2 for 'deliverable'?

    a)   Item ☐

    b)   Package ☐

    c)   Product ☐

    d)   Component ☐

9.   Which of these items does NOT involve the Project Board?

    a)   Exception Assessment ☐

    b)   Highlight Reports ☐

    c)   Project Closure ☐

    d)   Work Package Authorisation ☐

10. What name is given to the permissible deviation from a plan allowed without immediate reporting to the Project Board?

    a)   Allowance   ☐

    b)   Contingency   ☐

    c)   Concession   ☐

    d)   Tolerance   ☐

11. What other control is closely linked with configuration management?

    a)   Risk Management   ☐

    b)   Project Closure   ☐

    c)   Change Control   ☐

    d)   Project Initiation   ☐

12. Which of these processes does NOT trigger the Planning (PL) process?

    a)   Starting Up a Project (SU)   ☐

    b)   Initiating a Project (IP)   ☐

    c)   Managing Stage Boundaries (SB)   ☐

    d)   Controlling a Stage (CS)   ☐

13. In a Product Breakdown Structure what category of product is a Highlight Report?

    a)   Quality   ☐

    b)   Specialist   ☐

    c)   Technical   ☐

    d)   Management   ☐

14. If, after a Quality Review Follow-up Action, an error is still not resolved, what action should be taken?

    a)   An Exception Report is made   ☐

    b)   A Project Issue is raised   ☐

    c)   An Exception Memo is raised   ☐

    d)   The review is reconvened   ☐

15.   Which of the following is NOT a PRINCE2 definition of a project?

   a)   Has an organisation structure   ☐

   b)   Produces defined and measurable business products   ☐

   c)   Uses a defined amount of resources   ☐

   d)   Uses a defined set of techniques   ☐

16.   What environment does PRINCE2 assume?

   a)   A fixed-price contract   ☐

   b)   A Customer/Supplier environment   ☐

   c)   A specialist environment   ☐

   d)   A third-party environment   ☐

17.   Which feature of PRINCE2 tells the Project Manager where a product is,
      what its status is and who is working on it?

   a)   Work Package   ☐

   b)   Product Description   ☐

   c)   Checkpoint Report   ☐

   d)   Configuration management   ☐

18.   In 'Closing a Project' (CP) the project files are archived. What is the explanation
      given for this?

   a)   To provide useful lessons to future projects   ☐

   b)   Never throw anything away   ☐

   c)   This material may be needed by Programme Management   ☐

   d)   To permit any future audit of the project's actions   ☐

19.   Which of the following statements is FALSE? Project Managers using PRINCE2
      are encouraged to …

   a)   establish terms of reference as a prerequisite to the start of the project   ☐

   b)   use a defined structure for delegation, authority and communication   ☐

   c)   divide the project into manageable Stages for more accurate planning   ☐

   d)   provide brief reports to Management at regular meetings   ☐

20.   Which of these is NOT a valid Risk Management action?

    a)   Prevention   ☐

    b)   Denial   ☐

    c)   Reduction   ☐

    d)   Transference   ☐

21.   Which one of these is NOT a PRINCE2 Component?

    a)   Plans   ☐

    b)   Controls   ☐

    c)   Work Package   ☐

    d)   Configuration management   ☐

22.   Which document lists the major products of a plan with their key delivery dates?

    a)   Product Outline   ☐

    b)   Product Breakdown Structure   ☐

    c)   Checkpoint Report   ☐

    d)   Product Checklist   ☐

23.   The configuration of the final deliverable of the project is:

    a)   the sum total of its products   ☐

    b)   the interim products   ☐

    c)   its product description   ☐

    d)   the single end-product   ☐

24.   Which part of a product lifespan is not part of a project life cycle in the eyes of PRINCE2?

    a)   The change-over to operational use of the product   ☐

    b)   Assessment of the value of the product after a period of use   ☐

    c)   The specification of the product   ☐

    d)   Finalisation of the Business Case   ☐

25.   What is the first job carried out on receipt of a new Project Issue?

    a)   Allocation of priority   ☐

    b)   Logging   ☐

    c)   Decision on what type of issue   ☐

    d)   Impact Analysis   ☐

26.   Which of these statements is FALSE?

    a)   The Project Plan is an overview of the total project   ☐

    b)   For each stage identified in the Project Plan, a Stage Plan is required   ☐

    c)   An Exception Plan needs the approval of the next higher level of authority   ☐

    d)   A Team Plan needs approval by the Project Board   ☐

27.   Which of the following statements is FALSE?

    a)   Customer quality expectations should be discovered in the process 'Starting Up a Project'   ☐

    b)   A company's QMS becomes part of PRINCE2   ☐

    c)   PRINCE2 may form part of a company's QMS   ☐

    d)   The Stage Plan describes in detail how part of the Project Plan will be carried out   ☐

28.   Which one of these statements describes the true purpose of Acceptance Criteria?

    a)   A justification for undertaking the project based on estimated costs and anticipated benefits   ☐

    b)   A measurable definition of what must be done for the final product to be acceptable to the Customer   ☐

    c)   To provide a full and firm foundation for the initiation of a project   ☐

    d)   To trigger 'Starting Up a Project'   ☐

29.   How often does PRINCE2 recommend that open Project Issues should be reviewed?

    a)   Weekly   ☐

    b)   At Exception Assessments   ☐

    c)   At Checkpoint Meetings   ☐

    d)   On a regular basis   ☐

30.　What other product is reviewed at the end of each stage apart from
　　　the Business Case and Project Plan?

　　　a)　　The Project Mandate　☐

　　　b)　　The Quality Log　☐

　　　c)　　The Risk Log　☐

　　　d)　　The Project Brief　☐

31.　Why is a copy of the Project Issue always returned to the author?

　　　a)　　The author owns it　☐

　　　b)　　To acknowledge its receipt and entry into the system　☐

　　　c)　　To elicit further information　☐

　　　d)　　To notify rejection of the Issue　☐

32.　Which product reviews the benefits achieved by the project?

　　　a)　　Post-Project Review　☐

　　　b)　　Post-Project Review Plan　☐

　　　c)　　End Project Report　☐

　　　d)　　Follow-on Action Recommendations　☐

33.　Which of these statements is FALSE?

　　　a)　　A PRINCE2 project has a finite lifespan　☐

　　　b)　　A PRINCE2 project has a defined amount of resources　☐

　　　c)　　A PRINCE2 project may have only activities, i.e. no products　☐

　　　d)　　A PRINCE2 project has an organisation structure with defined
　　　　　　responsibilities, to manage the project　☐

34.　The person best situated to keep an eye on a risk is called its …?

　　　a)　　Supporter　☐

　　　b)　　Monitor　☐

　　　c)　　Owner　☐

　　　d)　　Librarian　☐

35. Which document reviews actual achievements against the Project Initiation Document?

    a)   End Project Report ☐

    b)   Post-Project Review ☐

    c)   Lessons Learned Report ☐

    d)   Follow-on Action Recommendations ☐

36. In PRINCE2 all potential changes are dealt with as …?

    a)   Configuration items ☐

    b)   Requests for Change ☐

    c)   Project Issues ☐

    d)   Exception Reports ☐

    e)   Action items ☐

37. Which one of these is NOT a key criterion for producing a Product Flow Diagram?

    a)   Are the products clearly and unambiguously defined? ☐

    b)   On what other products is each product dependent? ☐

    c)   Is any product dependent on a product outside the scope of this plan? ☐

    d)   Which products can be developed in parallel? ☐

38. For a Quality Review, when are suitable reviewers identified?

    a)   When the product is passed to configuration management ☐

    b)   In the Project Quality Plan ☐

    c)   During the QR preparation step ☐

    d)   In planning the relevant stage ☐

39. The existence of what product is checked in 'Starting Up a Project' and its initial version finalised in 'Initiating a Project'?

    a)   The Project Mandate ☐

    b)   The Project Plan ☐

    c)   The Project Brief ☐

    d)   The Business Case ☐

40.   Which does PRINCE2 regard as the third project interest, given user and
       supplier as the other two?

       a)   Technical   ☐

       b)   Management   ☐

       c)   Business   ☐

       d)   Quality   ☐

41.   PRINCE2 lists a number of reasons why it is seldom desirable or possible to plan
       an entire project in detail at the start. Which of these is NOT one of these reasons?

       a)   A changing or uncertain environment   ☐

       b)   A PRINCE2 requirement   ☐

       c)   Difficulty in predicting business conditions in the future   ☐

       d)   Difficulty in predicting resource availability well into the future   ☐

42.   In which process is the Project Brief produced?

       a)   Starting Up a Project   ☐

       b)   Initiating a Project   ☐

       c)   Authorising Initiation   ☐

       d)   Authorising a Project   ☐

43.   When should a Product Description be baselined?

       a)   As soon as it is available in draft form   ☐

       b)   When the associated product has passed its quality check   ☐

       c)   When the plan containing its creation is baselined   ☐

       d)   As soon as it is written   ☐

44.   An Exception Plan covers what period?

       a)   From the problem to the end of the project   ☐

       b)   From the problem to the end of a plan that will no longer finish within
             agreed tolerances   ☐

       c)   The work needed to put the project back within its tolerances   ☐

       d)   The time needed to produce an Exception Report   ☐

45. Stage boundaries may be chosen according to a number of parameters.
Which one of the following is NOT one of the parameters?

    a)   The need to have a separate stage for the formal close of the project ☐

    b)   A review of a risky project at key moments when new information about those risks appears ☐

    c)   Ensuring that key decisions are made prior to the detailed work needed to implement them ☐

    d)   Providing a 'fire break' for the project by encouraging the Project Board to assess the project viability at regular intervals ☐

46. The initial Project Plan is based on the Project Brief, the Project Quality Plan and which other product?

    a)   The Project Approach ☐

    b)   The Project Initiation Document ☐

    c)   The project start-up notification ☐

    d)   The Project Mandate ☐

47. Which document is a record of some current or forecast failure to meet a requirement?

    a)   Exception Report ☐

    b)   Off-Specification ☐

    c)   Follow-on Action Recommendations ☐

    d)   Highlight Report ☐

48. If there is a request to change a baselined product, and the change can be done within the stage or Work Package tolerances, how can the decision to implement the change be made?

    a)   Project Manager's decision ☐

    b)   Team Manager's decision ☐

    c)   Team member's decision to whom the work has been allocated ☐

    d)   Formal change control ☐

49. 'Controlling a Stage' drives which other process on a frequent, iterative basis?

    a)   Managing Stage Boundaries ☐

    b)   Approving a Stage or Exception Plan ☐

     c)   Managing Product Delivery   ☐

     d)   Planning   ☐

50.   The Project Quality Plan is written in which process?

     a)   Initiating a Project   ☐

     b)   Starting Up a Project   ☐

     c)   Managing Stage Boundaries   ☐

     d)   Directing a Project   ☐

51.   What are defined as 'partitions of the project with decision points'?

     a)   Work Packages   ☐

     b)   Product Descriptions   ☐

     c)   Quality Reviews   ☐

     d)   Stages   ☐

52.   In which lower-level process of 'Controlling a Stage' is the Risk Log updated?

     a)   Reporting Highlights   ☐

     b)   Assessing Progress   ☐

     c)   Capturing Project Issues   ☐

     d)   Examining Project Issues   ☐

53.   If a question arises on why a particular product was changed, which element of PRINCE2 would be of most help in finding the information?

     a)   Issue Log   ☐

     b)   Quality Log   ☐

     c)   Configuration Management   ☐

     d)   Change Control   ☐

54.   In which sub-process is a Stage Plan updated with actuals?

     a)   Assessing Progress   ☐

     b)   Reviewing Stage Status   ☐

     c)   Planning a Stage   ☐

     d)   Reporting Highlights   ☐

55. In which sub-process are Checkpoint Reports created?

   a) Executing a Work Package ☐

   b) Assessing Progress ☐

   c) Reporting Highlights ☐

   d) Reviewing Stage Status ☐

56. Are the following statements true or false?

   – Delegated Project Assurance roles report directly to corporate or programme management

   – In PRINCE2 the Project Manager role must be full time

   – A project management structure is a temporary structure

   a) All three are false ☐

   b) Only the third is true ☐

   c) Only the first is false ☐

   d) The second and third are false ☐

57. The process, 'Directing a Project' begins when?

   a) From 'Starting Up a Project' ☐

   b) After the start-up of the project ☐

   c) At the end of the Initiation Stage ☐

   d) Before start-up of the project ☐

58. Apart from 'Initiating a Project', in which process is the Business Case updated?

   a) Managing Product Delivery ☐

   b) Controlling a Stage ☐

   c) Managing Stage Boundaries ☐

   d) Authorising a Stage ☐

59. The existence of what information is expected by the process 'Starting up a Project'?

   a) A Project Plan ☐

   b) A Project Mandate ☐

   c) An appointed organisation ☐

   d) Project Initiation Document ☐

60. In the PRINCE2 document management structure, how many types of file are recommended?

    a)   One for each Stage   ☐

    b)   Two; Management and Specialist   ☐

    c)   Just the Quality File   ☐

    d)   Three; Project, Stages and Quality   ☐

61. In a quality review which role does PRINCE2 suggest must ensure that all reviewers are provided with the relevant review products?

    a)   Producer   ☐

    b)   Scribe   ☐

    c)   Review Chairperson   ☐

    d)   Configuration Librarian   ☐

62. Which of these is mandatory in a PRINCE2 project?

    a)   The use of Team Managers   ☐

    b)   The use of Exception Plans   ☐

    c)   The use of Stages   ☐

    d)   The use of quality reviews   ☐

63. The Project Board has three responsibilities towards the management of risk. Which of the following options is the FALSE one?

    a)   Notifying the Project Manager of any external risk exposure to the project   ☐

    b)   Making decisions on recommended reactions to risk   ☐

    c)   Identifying, recording and regularly reviewing risks   ☐

    d)   Striking a balance between levels of risk and potential benefits   ☐

64. What function creates, maintains and monitors the use of a quality system?

    a)   Project Support   ☐

    b)   Quality Planning   ☐

    c)   Quality Control   ☐

    d)   Quality assurance   ☐

65. Which is not a purpose of configuration management?

a)   To identify products ☐

b)   To create products ☐

c)   To track products ☐

d)   To protect products ☐

66. Which step is NOT part of 'Accepting a Work Package'?

a)   Understand the reporting requirements ☐

b)   Agree tolerance margins for the Work Package ☐

c)   Monitor and control the risks associated with the Work Package ☐

d)   Produce a Team Plan which shows that the Work Package can be completed within the constraints ☐

67. Which process provides the information needed for the Project Board to assess the continuing viability of the project?

a)   Starting Up a Project ☐

b)   Closing a Project ☐

c)   Planning ☐

d)   Managing Stage Boundaries ☐

68. In which process are choices made about planning tools and estimating methods?

a)   Starting Up a Project ☐

b)   Initiating a Project ☐

c)   Managing Stage Boundaries ☐

d)   Planning ☐

69. In which process are decisions made on Exception Reports?

a)   Managing Stage Boundaries ☐

b)   Closing a Project ☐

c)   Directing a Project ☐

d)   Managing Product Delivery ☐

70. Which process checks for changes to the project management team?

   a)   Starting Up a Project   ☐

   b)   Managing Stage Boundaries   ☐

   c)   Closing a Project   ☐

   d)   Directing a Project   ☐

71. From the products listed, which one is produced during 'Starting Up a Project'?

   a)   The Project Initiation Document   ☐

   b)   The Project Plan   ☐

   c)   The Project Quality Plan   ☐

   d)   The Project Approach   ☐

72. Quality responsibilities, both within and external to the project, are defined in which process?

   a)   Initiating a Project   ☐

   b)   Starting Up a Project   ☐

   c)   Managing Stage Boundaries   ☐

   d)   Directing a Project   ☐

73. Acceptance for the completed products is obtained as part of which process?

   a)   Closing a Project   ☐

   b)   Managing Product Delivery   ☐

   c)   Managing Stage Boundaries   ☐

   d)   Controlling a Stage   ☐

74. An Exception Report is produced in which sub-process?

   a)   Taking Corrective Action   ☐

   b)   Reviewing Stage Status   ☐

   c)   Escalating Project Issues   ☐

   d)   Reporting Highlights   ☐

75.   Which is the missing section of the suggested Project File, if the others are
       Organisation, Plans, Business Case, Communication Plan and Control?

       a)   Correspondence ☐

       b)   Daily Log ☐

       c)   Risk Log ☐

       d)   Issue Log ☐

       e)   PID ☐

Total Score:

Marking your paper

Now you have completed the sample Foundation Examination paper, check your answers
against those shown in the following table and look up the page number references in the
manual for any questions you answered incorrectly. Table 1A shows the page numbers in the
2002 edition of the manual. Table 1B gives the page numbers from the 2005 edition. You
should, ideally, be looking for a score of between 60–65 correct answers and completion
within 40–50 minutes. Remember, for the actual examination you need to score 38 correct
answers in 60 minutes.

Table 1A Answer sheet

Q	Answer	Page	Q	Answer	Page	Q	Answer	Page
1	B	6	26	D	213/214	51	D	234
2	D	312	27	B	254	52	D	106
3	C	168/169	28	B	309	53	C	270
4	D	7	29	D	105	54	A	101
5	B	37/38	30	C	141	55	A	128
6	D	229	31	B	297	56	B	39
7	C	149	32	A	233	57	A	67
8	C	311	33	C	7	58	C	193
9	D	98	34	C	241	59	B	26
10	D	222	35	A	159	60	B	393
11	C	275	36	C	295	61	A	301
12	D	165	37	A	288	62	C	234
13	D	281	38	D	259	63	C	241
14	B	306	39	D	37	64	D	254
15	D	7	40	C	198	65	B	263
16	B	195	41	B	213	66	C	126
17	D	263/264	42	A	37	67	D	134
18	D	154	43	C	284	68	D	167
19	D	3	44	B	215	69	C	85
20	B	244	45	A	237	70	B	136
21	C	187	46	A	51	71	D	27/39
22	E	184	47	B	295	72	A	49
23	A	263	48	D	295	73	B	124
24	B	8	49	C	94	74	C	117
25	B	272	50	A	49	75	C	393

Table 1B Answer sheet

Q	Answer	Page	Q	Answer	Page	Q	Answer	Page
1	B	6	26	D	225	51	D	246
2	D	315	27	B	266	52	D	108
3	C	54	28	B	329	53	C	282
4	D	7	29	D	108	54	A	103
5	B	37/38	30	C	15	55	A	133
6	D	120	31	B	317	56	B	205
7	C	153	32	B	246	57	A	69
8	C	331	33	C	7	58	C	137
9	D	98	34	C	253	59	B	26
10	D	339	35	A	163	60	D	421
11	C	282	36	C	315	61	A	321
12	D	13	37	A	302/3	62	C	246
13	D	297	38	D	272/326	63	C	253
14	B	325	39	D	201	64	D	266
15	D	7	40	C	206	65	B	275
16	B	203	41	B	223	66	C	130
17	D	276	42	A	26	67	D	15
18	D	158	43	C	300	68	D	171
19	D	3	44	B	225	69	C	87
20	B	256	45	A	247	70	B	138
21	C	195	46	A	53	71	D	27
22	D	174	47	B	315	72	A	51
23	A	275	48	D	282	73	B	136
24	B	8	49	C	96	74	C	121
25	B	286	50	A	50	75	C	421

The Practitioner Examination

You must have passed the PRINCE2 Foundation Examination in order to sit the Practitioner Examination.

The Practitioner Examination is a three-hour, open-book examination. Under current rules, you may take the PRINCE2 manual and any notes (including this book) into the examination. A computer or any other electronic reference material is not allowed at present.

On 4 October 2002 a new style of Practitioner Examination paper was introduced as part of continuous efforts to improve the effectiveness of the examination. The following paragraphs explain this format, indicating the different types of question now being asked, and some suggestions on how to structure answers most appropriately.

The objective of the exam remains the same – to enable a candidate to demonstrate to the examiner an understanding of PRINCE2 and an ability to apply the methodology in an appropriate way in a given set of circumstances described in a scenario.

Structure of the paper

The examination paper will consist of a scenario – no more than one page of A4. There may also be one or two attachments, each one augmenting the scenario information, and being associated with a particular question.

The combination of the scenario, each question and any attachment will always 'position' both the candidate (to consider a particular PRINCE2 role) and the project (in terms of the timescale, e.g. at the beginning, in the middle or at the end of a project). The role to be considered will be at a level suitable for a project manager or one who is aiming to become a project manager.

There are three questions, each worth 50 marks. This gives a total of 150 marks. The pass mark is 75. Some or all of the three questions may be divided into parts. Where this is the case, the portion of the 50 marks allocated to each part will be shown. All questions and part questions should be answered.

PRINCE2 topics commonly addressed

The guidance in the OGC publication, *Managing Successful Projects with PRINCE2*, which addresses the processes, components and techniques of PRINCE2, forms the basis for all the examination questions. Within that broad framework, topics typically examined are:

- The Business Case – create a Business Case or comment on an offered poor example of one.

- Controls – often focused on specific roles or timeframe within a project.

- Monitoring and control of project work by either the Project Board or the Project Manager.

- Organisation – structures and roles, often asking for suggested appointments for the scenario project.

- Plans – structures, types and levels, their benefits, the creation of a Product Breakdown Structure and Product Flow Diagram.

- Risk – analysis of a risk.

- Quality – throughout the project life cycle or focused on a specific period of the scenario.

- Configuration management – the role of the Configuration Librarian, the link with Change Control.

- Work Packages – the creation of one.

- Tolerances – understanding them, writing an Exception Report.

- Project Issues – understanding the flow, doing an impact analysis.

- Project closure – understanding the sub-processes and products, handling open issues and risks, premature close.

Types of question

Questions are categorised as analytical, contextual or theoretical. Occasionally a question may be a combination of two of these categories. The examination paper will not state the type of question.

Analytical questions

Questions in this category may require any of the following:

- Specific PRINCE2 products to be created

- Comments or recommendations to be made about a PRINCE2 product that is provided as an attachment

- Information from the scenario and an attachment to be used in answering the question.

Contextual questions

Questions in this category enable candidates to demonstrate an understanding of how various PRINCE2 topics are linked and might be applied in the circumstances described in the scenario. An example here might be to ask where the Risk Log is updated.

Theoretical questions

Questions in this category provide a means of enabling candidates to demonstrate an understanding of the theory and philosophy of various PRINCE2 topics.

Great care is taken to try to balance the exam papers in terms of level of difficulty and type of questions.

Wording of questions

Typically, the questions will ask the candidates to 'identify', 'explain', 'describe', 'comment on', 'list', 'draw', 'create', 'summarise', 'write', 'draft' or 'write notes on' (a particular

PRINCE2 document). An alternative style of question is 'How would you/PRINCE2…?' The question may require the candidate to base the answer on one or more aspects of PRINCE2, e.g. processes, components, techniques or management products. The section below addresses how the answers to questions should be tackled.

Questions will make it clear whether they are asking candidates to identify processes (SU, IP) or sub-processes (SU1, IP3). Candidates may choose to use the identifier, write out the sub-process name in full or give a full description of it. Where you are asked to identify actions, such as stating that the Project Board allocates stage tolerances to the Project Manager, always mention in which sub-process these things are done.

Answering the questions

The first fifteen minutes (reading time) of the exam is intended to allow the candidate to absorb all the information provided. The invigilator is only allowed to explain a word or phrase whose meaning is difficult for a delegate taking the exam in a language other than their first language. The invigilator is not allowed to relate a question to the PRINCE2 aspects involved. After this period, there are three hours in which to answer the questions. Years of experience tells us it is necessary to remind candidates – **read the question, answer the question**. It does sometimes appear that the candidate has not done one or the other – or both!!

The candidate's answer, when passed to the examiner, is the only means by which a judgement can be reached on whether the candidate knows and understands the aspects of PRINCE2 being examined. Examiners have no access to the candidate name, training company, or even whether a training course has been attended – candidates are simply identified by a number.

Clear, legible handwriting is a blessing to the examiner! Every effort is made to read what the candidate has written, but if it cannot be read, it cannot be marked.

Structuring the answer

Try to answer requests for explanations or summaries in bullet points with one or two short sentences of explanation. You are allowed to answer in essay form, but please remember that this takes a lot of your time. You are not marked on your prose, only on your PRINCE2 knowledge. If what you are thinking of writing does not make a PRINCE2 point, don't write it. Remember that it is a PRINCE2 exam, not a general project management exam.

Where lists are requested, lists should be created. If the number of items in that list is specified in the question, then only provide that number, not more. For example, if a question asks for six sub-processes that affect the Business Case, the first six listed by the candidate will be taken as the answer. Any extra ones will be **IGNORED**. If a question asks for **all** sub-processes, for example, where the Issue Log is studied, do not 'brain-dump' every sub-process of every process. If such a list contains many sub-processes that have nothing to do with the question asked, the marks available are halved.

When asked to draw a diagram, do just that. Do not explain when, by whom and why unless the question asks for this. An example here would be a request to draw product-based planning diagrams.

If asked to create a specific PRINCE2 document, look at the Composition section of the Product Description of that product. This will give you the sub-headings for the document. Do not write **about** the product, about who produces it, in what sub-process or why. Just create the document. If a different part of the question asks the other questions, then fine, give the other information then.

General advice

Fifty marks are available for each of the three questions, giving a total of 150. The requirement for passing the Practitioner Examination is that you must score at least 50% of the marks available, so 75 marks must be gained to achieve a pass. The marks are accumulated for all the questions so it is possible (but difficult) to compensate for one poorly answered question by a brilliant answer to another. Don't be tempted to spend 90–120 minutes on one question about which you feel comfortable. Questions are designed to be answerable in 50–60 minutes. Spending more than this brings in the law of diminishing returns, and you are likely to be spending 10–15 minutes describing in wonderful detail some point that is only worth 1 mark.

Do not use the term, 'etc.' in any answer. If there is more to say in answer to the question asked, write it down.

Don't repeat yourself.

Do not refer the examiner to a page in the manual.

Points made in one part of a question may earn marks for another part of the same question if it is clear that you understand the point required (e.g. a point made in answer to question 1B may reveal that the candidate knew a point for which marks were available in question 1A). Marks cannot cross question boundaries (e.g. from question 2 to question 1), because different questions address different aspects of the methodology. If a similar point needs making in another question, make it again.

Start each answer to a sub-question on a new page. This allows you to go back later and add to the answer to a previous question if you have time. You may wish to number your pages as, for example, Q1A–1, Q1A–2, starting from page 1 for each new sub-question. This makes it easier to add extra pages to a question's answer if you go back later.

Answer what to you are the easiest questions or sub-questions first to boost your feeling of confidence, but try not to go beyond the time allowance.

Analytical questions

These require the candidate to demonstrate the ability to apply a particular aspect of PRINCE2 to a set of circumstances described in the scenario, attachments or in the question.

Analytical questions may invite comment on a particular PRINCE2 product. Such products may be:

- An extract from a draft PID
- A Project Quality Plan
- A Quality Log
- A Product Flow Diagram (when compared to a provided Product Breakdown Structure)

This type of question may also require the candidate to create a PRINCE2 product, such as:

- Business Case
- Configuration Item Record
- Exception Report
- Highlight Report
- Product Description
- Project Approach
- Project Brief
- Project Issue
- Work Package

Contextual questions

Contextual questions test the understanding of the links between sub-processes and between components and sub-processes.

A contextual question might require a candidate to list the sub-processes in which a particular PRINCE2 product might be used, e.g. in which sub-processes is the Business Case reviewed.

Theoretical questions

These are straightforward questions on information held either in the manual or course notes. They will test the understanding of the PRINCE2 philosophy and principles. An example of a theoretical question might be to explain the benefits of using the levels of plan proposed by PRINCE2 or why the Business Case is considered as the driving force of a PRINCE2 project.

The problems

Since the introduction of the original PRINCE2 Professional Examinations in January 1997, most of the failures (about 35%) have stemmed from the Practitioner Examination. The reasons are varied, with some candidates simply running out of time and failing to score sufficient marks for the final question. Many failed to answer the question posed (and produced an answer that was easier to write but irrelevant!) or were unable to make the all-important connections between the scenario, the question, their experience and the PRINCE2 method.

Sometimes there is little doubt that candidates who fail actually understand the method. Many who fail are sensible middle-managers with at least some practical experience of project management. So the conclusion is that the problems lie with:

- time management
- information retrieval
- examination technique.

Reading time

Under current APM Group rules, candidates for the Practitioner Examination are allowed 15 minutes reading time. During this period you are not allowed to look up or write anything. You will be allowed to highlight and to make notes on the examination question paper and the special note pad provided. You will *not* be allowed to refer to the PRINCE2 reference manual, start your answers, leave the room or discuss the paper with the invigilator or other candidates.

Use the reading time carefully. Highlight the relevant points the scenario is making. You should aim to fully understand the background and the questions by the time the examination starts.

When reading the questions, underline the verbs to ensure you understand what the question is asking you to do. For example you might be asked to **create** a particular plan or diagram; or the question might ask you to **explain** or **describe** a particular element of PRINCE2. Remember, many candidates who fail the Practitioner Examination do so because they have not answered the question posed.

Time management

Do not waste valuable time repeating the question.

Beside each sub-question is the number of marks available for it. Take a rough allocation of fifty minutes for each question, and then break that down into the time that it is worth spending on each sub-question. For example, if a sub-question is worth only 5 marks, it is worth one-tenth of the fifty minutes (5 minutes) of your time to answer it. So each mark is worth 1 minute of your time.

To ensure that the best use is made of the time available; a reasonable approach is to aim for 'a mark per minute' allowing about 50 minutes to be allocated to each question. This should enable you sufficient time to score around 30–40 marks per question, which is about as many as you can reasonably expect under examination conditions. The questions will indicate a breakdown of the marks available for each part, so allocation of writing time to each part of the question, based on a 'mark per minute' will not be difficult.

But you must be disciplined!

Always leave time to read through your work. This will often reveal missing references and possibly missing key points. Allow about 15 minutes for this – if you find any major omissions and don't have time to write up the full text, just bullet-point the key features and you will be given marks for including them.

Sample Practitioner Examination Paper 1 (Effective from 1 July 2005)

Instructions

This paper is a compilation of a scenario, 5 questions and associated attachments. It is designed to provide ATOs and Practitioner Candidates a sample of the types of questions that may be asked.

Each question has a sample answer, which the examiners have prepared and, whilst these are not 'model' answers, they would score well if submitted.

Marking schemes have not been given as they change and without proper interpretation can be confusing. The candidates should be aware that no more than 2 marks are given for each point made.

As a guide, candidates should spend 1 minute of their time for each mark awarded, e.g. a 10 mark question would require the candidate to spend 10 minutes on the answer, a 25 mark question 25 minutes and so forth. This allows for 30 minutes planning and review time throughout the examination period.

Scenario

A large sweet-manufacturing company, Candy plc, has been at a disadvantage compared to its competitors due to its outdated technology and lack of control over its own marketing, and this is reflected in increasing costs and declining sales. Candy plc has decided to launch a new packaged, chocolate-covered, toffee bar to tackle the competition in the 'small bar' market. This will be handled as a PRINCE2 project and you are the Project Manager.

The Project Board consists of the Marketing Director (Senior User), Head of Production (Senior Supplier) and the Financial Director (Executive). An overall investment of £3.5m has been allocated for this venture, agreed by the Financial Director.

In the past Candy plc has sold direct to supermarket chains and wholesalers. The wholesalers sold the products on to small retailers. The supermarkets expected a lower price that gave them a 15% profit margin. Wholesaler and small retailers both expected a profit margin of 10%. This left Candy with a 15% profit margin. Marketing suggests that by going direct to the small retailers and offering a 12% profit margin, this would still provide Candy with a 25% profit margin. Sales to supermarkets would continue unchanged. For this product Candy plc will perform its own marketing and a new sales process is being developed within the project. The design and creation of the marketing material are needed for a comprehensive launch of the product. A decision is also needed on the target audience for the marketing material before it can be designed and distributed.

Candy plc needs to successfully launch the chocolate bar via direct sales while maintaining its current level of quality and customer satisfaction. The launch date is 2 January (8 months after the project start date). Breakeven point must be within

24 months of the launch. Marketing believe that direct sales will increase Candy plc's market share by 10%.

A feasibility study established that Candy could produce the new bar and its wrapping with current equipment, but recommended investment in new equipment at a cost of £250,000 that will allow production of the expected volumes for year 2 onwards. Using current equipment would require a night shift to produce the required volume at an additional cost of £185,000 per year.

To launch the product the project will generate an advertising campaign that will include both television and press advertisements. These will need to conform to corporate standards and include the corporate logo

The new production equipment needs to be ordered, delivered and installed. Agreements with suppliers need to be made for the provision of materials. These include the wrappers, boxed containers and the ingredients. The wrappers and boxes will need to comply with the size limits of the equipment. A trial of the production line will be needed, and sufficient supplies will need to be distributed to the sales outlets before the launch.

Question 1

(a)   There is a serious risk that the supplier of the production line equipment may not deliver the equipment on the date agreed (15th September).

Using the PRINCE2 approach carry out a risk analysis on this risk, giving your reasons for each step of the analysis. **(34 marks)**

(b)   Identify 8 sub-processes in which PRINCE2 states specifically that the Project Manager will examine risks and explain why the examination is done. **(16 marks)**

Question 2

Based upon your submission to the Project Board at the end of the start-up process, the initiation stage has been authorised. You are now in a position to plan the project. Using only the products in the scenario demonstrate your understanding of the project by drawing:

(a)   a Product Breakdown Structure for the project showing Specialist products only. **(20 marks)**

(b)   a Product Flow Diagram from the Product Breakdown Structure. **(30 marks)**

Note: no explanations of the diagrams are required.

Question 3

The project has moved on four months and is now in its final stage. See the attached memo from the Marketing Director (attachment 2). The Highlight Report (attachment 1), issued three weeks ago, is also for your information.

(a)   Draft the initial Issue Log entry for the production of miniatures. **(7 marks)**

(b)   Carry out an impact analysis based on the information available to you. **(22 marks)**

(c)   Assuming that after the impact analysis this change is confirmed as high priority, list the PRINCE2 processes you would use and what would be done in each to support this request. **(21 marks)**

Question 4

Assume that you have just entered the Initiation Stage. Using the information in the scenario and the extract from the Project Brief (attachment 3) write a Project Quality Plan using the headings stated within Appendix A of the PRINCE2 manual.
(40 marks)

Question 5

You are completing the assembly of the Project Initiation Document and have been passed the Business Case (attachment 4) for comment before you include it within the draft PID.

Using the information in attachment 5 and the scenario, review the attached Business Case, make comments on its content and add any suggestions you wish to make to improve its content. Exclude the Investment Appraisal from your considerations. **(50 marks)**

Attachment 1: Highlight Report

CANDY BAR PROJECT   7 October

To: Distribution List as per Communications Plan

Period Covered: 7 September to 7 October

Budget status

	Planned expenditure	Expenditure to date	Forecast total expenditure	Tolerance available
Project (£)	3.8m	3.4m	3.84m	0.1m
Stage (£)	0.6m	0.2m	0.64m	0.1m

Schedule status

	Planned end	Current forecast	Tolerance available
Project	7 January	7 January	Zero
Stage	7 January	7 January	Zero

Products completed during period

Marketing material

Installed equipment

Actual or potential problems and risk update

None

Products to be completed during the next period

Completed production trial

Distributed launch material

Launched Candy bar

Project issue status

None outstanding

Budget & schedule impact of any changes

Already has cost of £40,000 in overtime payments

Attachment 2: MEMO

From: The Marketing Director

To: The Project Manager

Date: October 28th

This morning I briefed my staff on the new Candy bar and how we will launch the product. During the briefing we received the results of some research that reveals that if we were to issue one box of miniature versions of the product as samples to go to all the shops in advance of the full marketing launch campaign, this would increase our customer base by 12%. The miniatures would be needed two weeks prior to the launch date. I have already had a word with the Production Director who pointed out that production of the miniatures would have to be done after the trial run. In elapsed time his senior engineer believes that it would need 4 weeks to modify the production line and 3 weeks to produce the miniatures. Marketing costs would rise by £75,000. Production costs would be £150,000. As there is no plan to produce the miniatures, I am raising this with you as a change that is urgently required. Could you please prepare the necessary paperwork for consideration?

Attachment 3: Extract from the Project Brief

Project Tolerances:

Time: The project is not required to complete before the 2nd January. A delay of 5 days is acceptable.

Cost: Plus / Minus £400,000 from the approved budget of £3.5m.

Scope: All areas should be covered. If Time/Cost is threatened then consideration can be given to delaying the installation of the new production line equipment for 6 months.

Benefit: Target increase in market share is 12% at 25% profit margin. Plus/minus 2% on both of these figures is acceptable.

Risk: There is no risk tolerance available on time. Risk may be taken on the other areas but must be discussed with the Executive before any decision is taken.

Quality: The bar must meet all the requirements of the Company Standards and be in line with Candy's other products, i.e. less than 1% rejects per production line run, averaged over a 2-month period.

            The bar must be acceptable to 90% of the Target Audience.

Customer's Quality Expectations:

The bar must be acceptable to the Target Audience.

The project must finish on the due date.

The expenditure must be in line with the budget.

The bar must conform to the Company Standards.

All products should be reviewed/tested to ensure conformance to the Product Descriptions.

Attachment 4: Business Case for inclusion in the PID

Reasons:

Candy needs to increase its market share and profit margin and has decided to launch a new Candy bar.

Options:

A number of options have been considered and Candy has chosen to implement a new Sales Process plus existing products, launch a new bar and install new equipment.

Benefits expected:

An increased market share and profit margin. Payback within 24 months.

Risks:

We may miss the end date and exceed the budget.

The figures may be incorrect.

Costs:

£3.4m

Timescales:

Must be implemented within 8 months.

Attachment 5: Supplementary Information

The feasibility study considered the following options:

1.   New Sales Process plus existing products and existing production line: Gives an increased profit margin of 25% but does not increase market share. Existing equipment may not be sustainable after 3 years.

2.   New Sales Process plus existing products, launch a new bar and use existing equipment: Gives an increased profit margin of 25%, an increase in market share of 12% but expected volumes cannot be sustained without night shift after year 2.

3.   New Sales Process plus existing products, launch a new bar and install new equipment: Gives an increased profit margin of 25%, an increase in market share of 12%, volumes can be sustained into year 2 and beyond without a night shift, saving £185,000 per annum in year 2 onwards. Additional less tangible benefits of decreased maintenance effort for the new equipment, improved staff morale as they see the company investing in their future.

4.   Do nothing: results in a continual decline and possible loss of jobs.

Chosen option: Option 3 as it gives the best long-term benefit and will enable the company to produce other new products in the future. This assumes that the competitors do not release similar products in the next 12 months and that the marketing predictions are accurate.

Sample Answer Question 1(a) – you should expect to spend about 34 minutes answering this question

There are four steps in Risk Analysis – Identify, Evaluate the Risk, Identify Suitable Responses, Select.

Identify:

There is a serious risk that the supplier of the production line equipment may not deliver the equipment on the date agreed (15th September).

This risk should be entered into the Risk Log, which will record the results of the analysis.

Category: This is a strategic/commercial risk (failure of suppliers to meet contractual commitments).

Evaluation:

Probability: Medium. Whilst delivery has been promised according to our requirements there is always a possibility that the supplier may have problems that may delay the delivery of the equipment.

Impact:

Time: High. The project cannot complete without the new equipment.

Quality: High. If the project does not complete then an Acceptance Criterion (target date) cannot be met.

Benefit: High. A delay in the project will mean the resulting benefits would be delayed. If the marketing material has been issued and we cannot satisfy the demand, the benefits may well be negative.

People/resources: Low. Morale may suffer if the production line is delayed.

Cost: Medium. It is likely that any delay will impact on costs. It may adversely affect our cost planning for the project. Resource costs will not stop during the delay.

Scope: High. If the delivery is late we will not be able to complete the scope of the project.

Proximity: September 15th.

Owner: The Senior Supplier (Head of Production). He is in a position to maintain a watching brief on the equipment supplier and could take the proposed actions.

Identify Suitable Responses:

Prevention: Cancel the order and use the existing equipment and the night shift – the risk can no longer happen.

Reduction: Order the equipment earlier to allow a longer delivery time for the supplier, thus less likely to happen; allow extra time in the plan for late delivery, thus reducing the impact; expedite the delivery weekly.

Transfer: Place liquidated damages in the contract thus encouraging the supplier to deliver on time; bonus the supplier for early/on time delivery, thus encouraging compliance with the delivery date.

Acceptance: We could hope for the best and accept the risk.

Contingency: Use the existing night shift until the new equipment arrives.

Selection:

This is based on the cost of taking action versus the cost of the risk occurring. It is very important that this project succeeds – however, it would seem that the new equipment is not definitely required to enable the initial benefits to be realised. Therefore I would recommend expediting the delivery, which will encourage the supplier to deliver on time *and* formulate a contingency plan using the existing equipment and a night shift. This has added benefits as the contingency plan can be used to mitigate a number of the risks associated with the new equipment, its delivery, installation and trial.

Sample Answer Question 1(b) – you should expect to spend about 16 minutes answering this question

Note the question asked for 8 processes so only 8 should be given.

The Project Manager will review the Risk Log during:

SU4 – Risk Log is created to record risks identified during SU – i.e. from the Mandate, during creation of the Project Brief, the Project Approach and the initiation Stage Plan.

IP3 – The Risk Log will be examined to ensure that any risks associated with the Business Case have been accurately recorded and analysed.

PL6 – During planning the Project, Stage or Team Plans a risk analysis will be conducted to ensure that the associated risks have been captured and analysed.

SB4 – The PM will review the Risk Log in its entirety at the end of the stage to ensure that all risks associated with the next stage have been captured and analysed, and that the risks associated with the stage coming to an end have been updated as necessary.

CS1 – Whilst negotiating and agreeing the Work Package with the Team Manager new risks may be identified or existing ones revised as part of this process.

CS4 – Whilst undertaking an impact analysis of a Project Issue the PM will investigate the effect on the risks – does the Project Issue give rise to new risks or affect existing risks? The Risk Log will be updated accordingly.

CS5 – During a review of the stage status the PM will review the risks associated with the period under review looking for any changes to the situation.

CS6 – The PM will include a review of the current risks in his/her Highlight Report to the Project Board.

Sample Answer: Q 2(a) – Product Breakdown Structure for the Launched Candy Bar Project – you should spend about 50 minutes answering all of Question 2

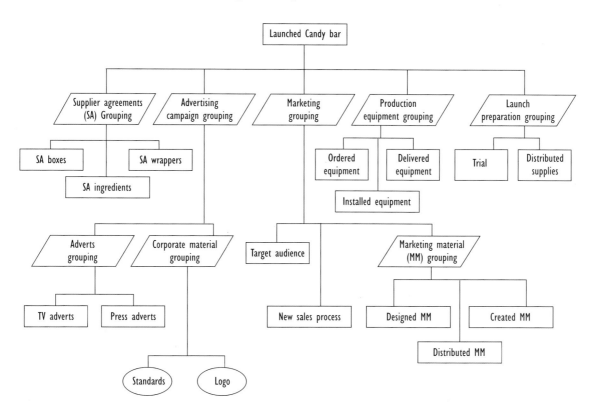

Sample Answer: Q 2(b) – Product Flow Diagram for the Launched Candy Bar Project

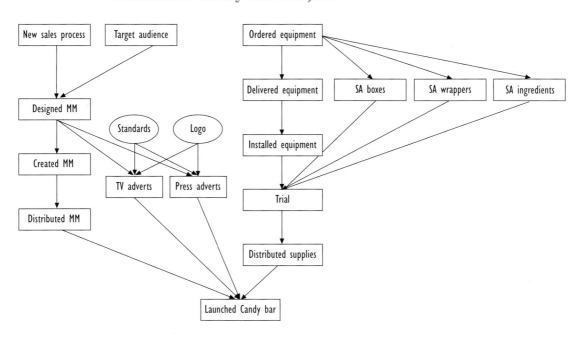

Sample Answer Question 3(a) – you should expect to spend about 7 minutes answering this question

Project Issue Number: 12
Type: Request For Change
Author: Marketing Director
Date Identified: October 28th
Date of Last Update: October 28th
Description: Research has shown a need to issue one box of miniature versions of the product as samples to go to all the shops in advance of the full marketing launch campaign.
Priority: 1
Status: Live, awaiting impact analysis.

Sample Answer Question 3(b) – you should expect to spend about 22 minutes answering this question

Impact Analysis

What would have to change?
The equipment would have to be changed in order to produce the miniatures.
Marketing material would have to change/be created for the miniatures.

What effort will the changes need?
The equipment change would take 4 weeks.
The production of the miniatures would take 3 weeks.
Production costs for the miniatures would be £150,000
Marketing costs would rise by £75,000.
No estimate is available at present for the extra time required by Marketing.

What is the impact on Project, Stage and Team Plans?
The work requires at least 9 weeks elapsed time to complete. There is about 10 weeks to go in the plan including Christmas so it is highly likely that these changes will delay completion of the project. Additionally, the extra costs involved are not included within the current budget.

What is the impact on Tolerance?
The combined costs would take both stage and project outside its current tolerance of £0.1m.
There is currently zero time tolerance, so the required time for the change would exceed time tolerances for both stage and project.

What is the impact on the Business Case?
Although the costs would rise, the expected profit margins would still provide a healthy, if reduced, Business Case. Further discussions with Marketing may be useful to provide more information about the forecasts.

What is the impact on the Risks?
Clearly the proposed change would put the current launch date at risk with knock-on effects to the timing of the TV and Press advertising, especially as contracts for these have already been signed.

There may be extra risks connected with packaging the miniatures. They would require new wrapping and boxes, which would lead to further costs and potential delay.

There is a further risk that the new production equipment may have problems in producing the miniatures, as it was never envisaged, when ordering the equipment, that we would be producing such a small size of bar.

Producing miniatures at this late stage on untested equipment may lead to quality problems. The production, packaging and boxing of the miniatures will have to be trialled.

Sample Answer Question 3(c) – you should expect to spend about 21 minutes answering this question

Assuming the Project Issue has now been raised, logged and the impact analysis done, I would escalate it to the Project Board by means of an Exception Report (CS8). This would define the change, list the options open, together with their impacts on plans, tolerances, the Business Case and risks, and contain my recommendation. The Project Board would study the report in DP4.

Because the change would exceed project time and cost tolerances, the decision would have to be referred to senior management by the Project Board. If the need for the change is accepted, I would be directed to create Exception Plans (SB6) to be presented for approval by the Project Board at an Exception Assessment. It is unlikely that the Project Board would order the premature close of the project (CP1-3), but would choose between implementing the change request, rejecting it or delaying either the launch or the issue of miniatures.

Implementation would cause new Work Packages to be created (CS1) or existing ones to be modified (CS7).

If the change is to be implemented, as the change exceeds Project Tolerance the new plans will have to be confirmed by the Corporate Body, more funds allocated and new Tolerances set at Project level.

Sample Answer Question 4 – you should expect to spend about 40 minutes answering this question

Project Quality Plan for the Candy Project

Customer Quality Expectations:

The bar must be acceptable to the Target Audience.

The project must finish on the due date.

The expenditure must be in line with the budget.

The bar must conform to the Company Standards.

All products should be reviewed/tested to ensure conformance to the Product Descriptions.

Quality Tolerances:

The bar must meet all the requirements of the Company Standards and be in line with Candy's other products, i.e. less than 1% rejects per production line run, averaged over a two-month period.

The bar must be acceptable to 90% of the Target Audience.

Acceptance Criteria:

Target Date: Complete by 7th January (includes tolerance).

Performance: 9 out of 10 people samples state that the new bar is satisfactory, 6 out of 10 samples state that the bar is better than satisfactory.

Development Cost: Should cost less than £3.9m including tolerance.

Major Functions: Must include a new sales process for small retailers, new production line equipment capable of meeting demand into year 2 and beyond.

Reliability: The new production line must produce bars with less than 1% rejects per run averaged over a two-month period.

Quality Responsibilities:

Executive: Must ensure that all the Acceptance criteria are met.

Senior User: Must ensure that Marketing products are to the standard required by the users.
Must sign off any product descriptions that may affect the users (such as new sales process, adverts, target audience).

Senior Supplier: Must ensure that all products produced meet the criteria laid down in the Product Descriptions.

Project Assurance (Executive): Ensure that all changes are monitored and approved. Ensure that project finance is being monitored appropriately.

Project Assurance (Senior User): Ensure that there is adequate and appropriate representation of the user at all reviews of the marketing products.

Project Assurance (Senior Supplier): Ensure that all supplier quality standards are being maintained. Ensure that all products produced have been adequately tested/inspected before delivery to the Customer.

Project Manager: Ensure that Product Descriptions are written and signed off. Ensure that Quality Reviews are planned and undertaken.

Team Managers: Ensure that Quality Reviews are undertaken and that the appropriate entries are made in the Quality Log.

Project Support: Act as a scribe in the Quality Review when appropriate. Ensure that the Quality Log is maintained. Act as Configuration Librarian (see below).

Reference to any standards that need to be met:

Development must conform to company standards.

All work must comply with current Health and Safety Regulations, standards and guidelines.

All work must comply with current Food and Hygiene standards.

Quality control and audit processes to be applied to project management:
Project Assurance will review the Project Manager's files at each stage boundary.

Project Assurance will review the Project Manager's draft plans prior to presentation to the Project Board.

Project Assurance will assist the Project Manager by reviewing any reports, memos etc. as required during the project.

Quality control and audit processes requirements for the specialist work:
All work will be reviewed in an appropriate manner (e.g. Quality Review Technique for documents, appropriate testing for the production line) at 'draft', 'interim' and 'final' points during production. The timing of these reviews/inspections/tests will be agreed between each supplier and the Project Manager when the Stage Plan is prepared. If the time between these reviews/inspections/tests is greater than 10 working days, further interim reviews/inspections/tests will be planned at times agreed between the Project Manager and the specialist supplier.

Change management procedures:
The Project Manager is authorised to accept small change requests that will not exceed in total 10% of the cost budget, each change being limited to a maximum of £1,000.

Any change greater than this amount, or one that will incur a delay to the project end date must be referred to the Executive for a decision.

Configuration Management Plan:
Product Storage:
Hard copies of all drawings, plans, specifications (and any other documentation) will be held in the project office. Soft copies of all information will be held on the project directory of the internal server.

File/retrieval Security:
Only the Configuration Librarian and the Project Manager will have write access to the projects directory.

The Configuration Librarian will issue copies of any information required by other team members.

Version Control:
All products will be identified using the standard scheme:

> Project id\Product Type\Product id\Version Number
> e.g. Candy Bar\Marketing\TV Advert\V1.0

Responsibilities:
The Configuration Librarian function will be handled by the company's administration team (to be identified).

Any tools to be used to ensure quality:
The PRINCE2 QR technique will be used for documents. The production line will be tested via a trial.

Sample Answer Question 5 – you should expect to spend about 50 minutes answering this question

The Business Case offered is inadequate in many respects.

Reasons

Comments:

The reason given is, in fact, a benefit and does not reflect the current situation.

Suggestions:

I would change the text to read: 'Candy plc has been at a disadvantage compared to its competitors due to its outdated technology and lack of control over its own marketing, and this is reflected in increasing costs and declining sales. To counteract this decline this project has been initiated.'

Options

Comments:

The statement does not state what other options have been considered. This will not give the readership (the Project Board in particular) confidence that this is the best option.

Suggestions:

I would change the text to read:

A number of options have been considered:

1. Implement a new sales process plus existing products and existing production line: Gives an increased profit margin of 25% but does not increase market share. Existing equipment may not be sustainable after 3 years.

2. Implement a new sales process plus existing products, launch a new bar and use existing equipment: Gives an increased profit margin of 25%, an increase in market share of 12% but expected volumes cannot be sustained without night shift after year 2.

3. Do nothing: results in a continual decline and possible loss of jobs.

4. Implement a new sales process plus existing products, launch a new bar and install new equipment.

    This is the chosen option as it gives the best long-term benefit and will enable the company to produce other new products in the future.

Benefits expected

Comments:

The benefits given are vague.

Suggestions:

I would change the text to read:

Increased profit margin of 25%

Increase in market share of 12%

Volumes can be sustained into year 2 and beyond without a night shift, saving £185,000 per annum in year 2 onwards.

Additional less tangible benefits of decreased maintenance effort for the new equipment, improved staff morale as they see the company investing in their future.

Payback within 24 months.

Risks
Comments:
The risks stated are in fact effects of other risks. More risks could have been identified.

Suggestions:
I would change the text to read:

The marketing projections may be inaccurate resulting in reduced/negative benefits.

We may choose the wrong target audience resulting in fewer sales and reduced/negative benefits.

The supplier may not deliver the equipment in time delaying the project and the receipt of benefit.

The new sales process may not work as planned resulting in lower sales and reduced/negative benefits.

The new sales process may upset the wholesalers and they may change suppliers and thus negate benefits.

The installation of the new production line may affect the existing quality of production by adversely affecting the existing product lines.

Costs
Comments:
Insufficient detail is given. The figure is incorrect.

Suggestions:
I would suggest:

An investment of £3.5m has been made with £250,000 set aside for the new production equipment. Breakeven point is expected within 24 months.

Timescales
Comments:
Could have more detail.

Suggestions:
I would reword as follows:

The project will take 8 months to implement and it is expected that this will be completed by 2nd January.

Sample Practitioner Examination Paper 3

Scenario

A very important project has just begun to implement a new sales process throughout the organisation (including job changes, procedures and computing). This follows a feasibility study that ended five months ago. This is the first project in the company to be run under PRINCE2. The Project Manager, who works for the IT manager, and the HO sales manager have both attended PRINCE2 courses and passed the exams. Senior management's knowledge of PRINCE2 is very little.

The project began a few weeks ago with the three teams currently gathering detailed requirements from the users. The Project Manager is inexperienced, but did a good job as one of the IT analysts who produced the feasibility study. In order to keep costs down, no Team Managers have been appointed. The three teams from IT, personnel and business process re-engineering all report to the Project Manager.

A Project Board has been appointed. The business process re-engineering manager, whose people will have to modify the manual procedures, is concerned that too many people are claiming to control different aspects of the project, and has raised this concern with the Sales Director. The Project Board has seventeen people on it. It consists of:

- The sales director, for whom the project is being done

- The accounts manager, who has been invited onto the Project Board because, although he has never done the job personally, he says he has experience in handling project managers

- Six branch managers, whose sales staff will be affected

- The business process re-engineering manager

- The personnel manager who will have to negotiate any job changes

- The IT manager whose staff will carry out the computing part of the work

- The head office sales manager, whose staff will be affected

- Two external marketing consultants, who advised the company on a recent marketing exercise

- The manager of internal audit

- Two senior sales representatives, who will personally be affected.

An organisation chart of the company is attached, showing the positions of the people mentioned in the scenario.

Because of the importance of the project, the Project Board is insisting on a progress meeting on the first Friday of every month. These take a whole day with all board members questioning the Project Manager about all aspects of the project, offering opinions about how to proceed and challenging work priorities. Because of the scope and intensity of the questioning, the Project Manager has to spend two or three days

Company Organisation Chart

in preparation for the meetings. This is a problem because the Project Manager still considers that he / she is the lead analyst and has allocated to himself / herself a full-time technical workload.

Also, the accounts manager and one of the senior sales representatives meet with the Project Manager at least once a week. In fact, the business process re-engineering manager has seen the accounts manager in the Project Manager's office several times a week. On being questioned about this, the Project Manager reported that the accounts manager always said he wanted to check work status, but was in effect trying to put pressure on the Project Manager to reduce the time allowed for activities.

The Project Manager is working from a plan created during feasibility. An IT consultant produced the plan, concentrating on what were estimated as the technical activities that would be required. The plan shows that the project will last fifteen months.

Questions

1(a) Suggest a revised Project Board, including who the members should be, what role they should take and the reasons for your choice. **(12 marks)**

1(b) Describe what roles should be given to those who you suggest should be removed from the Project Board, and the reasoning behind your proposals. **(24 marks)**

1(c) Is there any information in the scenario that suggests that the Project Manager's job might be a problem? If so, what measures would you suggest to improve the situation? **(14 marks)**

2(a) What comments do you have about the meetings mentioned in the scenario? **(28 marks)**

2(b) The Project Manager's job is clearly going to be very busy. How might the use of a Daily Log help the Project Manager? **(22 marks)**

3(a) Discuss whether the suggestions in the memo from the analyst about the user requirements are valid or not (see attachment). **(19 marks)**

3(b) What actions would you recommend that the Project Manager took about the memo from the analyst? **(31 marks)**

Memo

From: Analyst on the Sales Process Re-engineering Project

To: Project Manager

I am not going to finish the specification of the user needs this week. The senior sales clerks who were identified to advise me on the sales requirements have cancelled the last three meetings that I arranged with them. They say that they are too busy to provide me with the specification of their needs. Last time I complained to the Head Office Sales Manager, but he told me that it was my job and that I should just continue with it, even if the senior sales clerks were too busy to help.

At our last Checkpoint meeting you mentioned that you hadn't used any of our two weeks' time tolerances for the stage. Could we add that to my target date? If so, I think that I can create their specification from their feasibility documents, plus talking to some of the more junior sales staff, and just get the senior sales clerks to check these when I have finished.

Marking Scheme

Q1(a)	Project Board Composition		
1.	Executive – Sales Director (2) MD (1) Finance Director (1) Allow only one choice. Reasons for choice (2)	4	
2.	Senior Supplier role – BPR Manager, Personnel Manager & IT Manager (1 each) or CS Director (2) Reasons (2)	5	
3.	Senior User HO Sales Manager or Sales Director (1) Reasons (2)	3	
Q1(b)	Roles for those not selected for the new pmt		
4.	Accounts Manager – No role (2) or some of Executive's assurance role (2) Reasons (2)	6	
5.	7 branch managers & HO Sales Manager– Possible user committee meeting under HO sales manager's chairmanship (2) Team Managers (1) user assurance role (2) Reasons (2)	7	
6.	External marketing consultants - Best option would be no role (2) Possible user assurance (1) Reasons (2)	5	
7.	Manager of internal audit – assurance role (or one of his/her staff) (1) Reason (1)	2	
8.	2 senior sales representatives – Either user assurance or no role (2) Reasons (2)	4	
Q1(c)			
9.	100% effort as lead analyst does not leave time to do Project Manager job	2	
10.	Shouldn't use inexperienced Project Manager on a key project	2	
11.	Appoint TMs (2) Project Manager probably has no knowledge of 2 of the 3 teams work (2)	4	
12.	Current PM should drop tech role (2) or become a Team member (1) TM (1)	4	
13.	PM to be HO Sales Manager	2	
Extra			
	Total	**50**	
Q2(a)			
1.	Replace progress meetings (2) with Highlight Reports (1) Explanation (2)	5	
2.	Management by exception (2) tolerances (1) stage tolerances (1) explanation (2) tolerance elements (1 each to max 6)	13	
3.	Exception Report (1) content (1) CS8 (1) DP4 (1) Exception Plan (1) DP3 (1)	6	
4.	Drop meetings with Accounts Manager & Sales rep (2) Communication Plan (2)	4	
Q2(b)			
5.	Reminder to check with risk owner on risk status	2	
6.	Note to check on what is on critical path in the next week	2	
7.	Note to check on products due to complete in next few days	2	
8.	Reminder to check on Quality Log entries for any problems	2	
9.	Note to check on outstanding Project Issue impact analyses	2	
10.	Follow up on any outstanding Highlight Report problems/actions from other people	2	
11.	Chase activities that are slipping to see if plan modification can be avoided	2	
12.	Check on state of tolerances	2	
13.	Notes from discussions with TMs, Project Board members	2	
14.	Phone calls to be made	2	
15.	Communication Plan changes (1) Work Packages that need adjustment (1)	2	
Extra			
	Total	**50**	

Marking Scheme

Q3(a)			
1.	Should all time tolerance be used for this delay (Up to 3 marks for demonstration of understanding pros and cons)	3	
2.	5-month old feasibility study may be out of date for getting accurate user needs	2	
3.	Senior User is responsible for quality of user specification (2) and commitment of resources to do it (2) at last ESA (2)	6	
4.	User requirements from junior staff is dangerous (2) they may not know enough (2)	4	
5.	Getting check by senior sales clerks at end is too late (2) may cause delays if they find errors/omissions (2)	4	
Q3(b)			
6.	Informal discussion with Senior User to get commitment	2	
7.	Mention in next HR (2) CS6 (1) in section on Potential Problems (2) Look for pressure on Senior User from other Project Board members (2)	7	
8.	Raise Project Issue (2) Issue Log (1) CS3 (1) CS4 (1) impact analysis (1) CS2 (1) CS5 (1)	8	
9.	Put in Risk Log (2) CS8 (1) Exception Report (1) Explanation (1)	5	
10.	DP4 (1) Exception Plan (1) exception assessment (1) change WP (1) CS1 & MP1 (1 each)	6	
11.	General understanding of the gradual escalation process for the Project Manager	3	
Extra			
	Total	50	

And finally ...

If you've managed to get this far you are as ready for the PRINCE2 examinations as you are ever likely to be. It remains only to wish you the little bit of luck that we all need to make a success of any venture in life. If you are still not confident of your knowledge of PRINCE2 or your ability to convince an examiner that you are able to apply it to a given situation, you should consider attending an APM Group accredited training event and, perhaps, try to gain a little more experience in using the method.

Practising writing answers to typical project management situations, using the approaches suggested in this book will certainly help to prepare you for the examination and help develop your ability to respond to a problem using a structured method.

The sample scenario above can also be used to set yourself other questions – for example '*Describe how you would handle any changes required during the project*' and '*Write a Product Description for one of the products in your Product Breakdown Structure*'.

You can also use your own experience to generate a scenario and questions – this is sometimes the easiest way to start your preparation. Try to identify the key topics for each question first; then answer the questions (or at least some parts of them). Remember that you will not score all the marks for just identifying and explaining the PRINCE2 topic, but that you must relate the topic to the scenario.

Good luck with your preparation.

July 2005

Index